Contents

Some words are shown in bold, **like this**. You can find out what they mean by looking in the glossary.

Meet the dogs

This photo shows a basset hound, a golden retriever, and a chihuahua.

There are hundreds of different kinds of dogs. They come in different colours and sizes.

Newborn

6 weeks

2 months

Golden retrievers are very good as pet dogs.

This book tells you about the life of a **female** golden retriever. She has floppy ears and a long tail. She began life as a tiny puppy.

1 year

3 years

8 years

Newborn

Mother dogs lick their puppies as they are born.

The mother dog has given birth to a **litter**. The little **female** puppy is the last to be born. She has lots of brothers and sisters.

Newborn

6 weeks

2 months

Now the newborn puppy is clean and dry. She cannot see or hear but she can feel and smell. She smells her mother and the other puppies in the litter.

A puppy's paws look very big compared to its body size!

1 year

3 years

8 years

1 week

The puppy's pink nose has now turned black.

The puppy feeds on her mother's milk. She has to push her way through her brothers and sisters to find a **teat** to suckle from.

Newborn

6 weeks

2 months

The smallest puppy in a
litter is called the runt.

The puppies feed and grow bigger.
They still cannot stand but they
snuggle up together and sleep.

1 year

3 years

8 years

6 weeks

A puppy's eyes open when it is about 10 days old.

The puppy's eyes have opened and she can see and hear. Her legs are strong now and she plays and explores.

Newborn

6 weeks

2 months

Puppies play-fight and then cuddle up together for a nap.

She plays with her brothers and sisters. Sometimes she pretends to fight with one of them. In this way the puppies learn who is stronger.

1 year

3 years

8 years

2 months

Puppies should have their injections before they go outside.

A **vet** checks the puppy all over and gives her a special **injection**. The injection will protect her from catching illnesses.

Newborn

6 weeks

2 months

Dogs can smell better than they can see.

The puppy can now go outside for the first time. Everything is strange. The puppy has a good sense of smell and uses it to explore.

1 year

3 years

8 years

3 months

The dog leaves her mother and goes to a new owner. She begins to eat solid food now instead of milk. It contains meat and biscuit.

A new puppy needs a lot of looking after.

Newborn

6 weeks

2 months

It's good for a dog to feel happy around other dogs.

Food gives the dog **energy** and keeps her healthy. Exercise makes her muscles stronger. She plays with other dogs she meets outside.

1 year

3 years

8 years

1 year

Large, active dogs need lots of exercise.

The dog is now fully grown. She has lots of **energy**. When her owner throws a stick, she runs and brings it back.

Newborn

6 weeks

2 months

Retrievers can be **trained** to do tasks and help people. Some are specially trained to be guide dogs. They help people with sight problems find their way around.

Guide dogs make sure it is safe for their owner to cross the road.

1 year

3 years

8 years

3 months later

This vet is listening to the dog's heart sounds and breathing.

It is time for the dog to go to the **vet** again. The vet makes sure that she is healthy.

Newborn

6 weeks

2 months

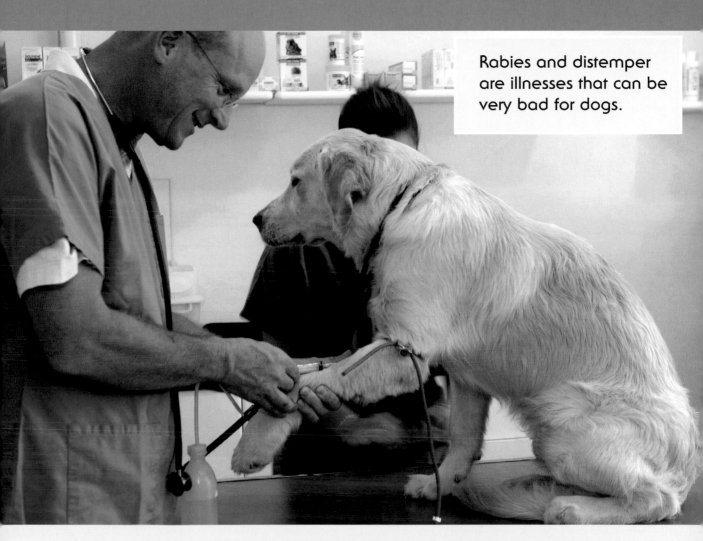

Rabies and distemper are illnesses that can be very bad for dogs.

A vet will give the dog a **booster injection** to make sure she does not get ill. The vet will also clip the dog's nails so they do not get too long.

1 year

3 years

8 years

3 years

Male and female golden retrievers look very similar. Males are usually a bit bigger.

The dog's owner wants her to have puppies of her own. She is taken to meet a **male** dog and they **mate**.

Newborn

6 weeks

2 months

Puppies are ready to be born about 63 days after mating.

Now several new puppies are growing inside her. Look how big her stomach is! She is almost ready to give birth.

1 year

3 years

8 years

9 weeks after mating

Puppies in the same litter are called litter-mates.

She gives birth to her **litter** of puppies one by one. The puppies are very small. They feed on her milk and grow quickly.

Newborn

6 weeks

2 months

The coats on golden retriever puppies get longer as they get older.

By the time they are three weeks old the puppies can bark and wag their tails. At three months old the puppies are ready to go to new owners.

1 year

3 years

8 years

5 years

Golden retrievers may go white around the face as they get older.

The dog misses her puppies for a few days, but then she forgets about them. She goes back to her old life with her owners.

Newborn

6 weeks

2 months

Golden retrievers like to swim and play in water.

The dog's owners take her for long walks. When they throw a stick she runs after it. She may swim through water to fetch the stick.

1 year

3 years

8 years

It's a dog's life

An older dog may need special food to keep it from gaining weight.

The dog is eight years old now. She still needs exercise every day, but she walks more slowly now and does not run about as before.

Newborn

6 weeks

2 months

Most dogs live until they are ten to fifteen years old. Small dogs often live longer than bigger dogs.

A dog can be your friend for a long time.

1 year

3 years

8 years

Life cycle

Newborn

6 weeks

2 months

1 year

3 years

8 years

Fact file

- Dogs are a **popular** pet. There are more than 7.3 million pet dogs in the United Kingdom.

- Retrievers have a waterproof undercoat. They like being in water.

- A dog has such a good sense of smell, it can smell and track people from the footprints left by their shoes.

- Retrievers can have several **litters**. In each litter they usually have seven to nine puppies.

Glossary

booster second injection to make the first injection work better

energy ability to run around and do things

female girl

guide dog dog that is trained to help people with sight problems find their way around

injection special liquid that is squirted into the body to help prevent an illness

litter several baby animals born together

male boy

mate come together (a male and a female) to produce babies

popular liked by many people

teat female's nipple that puppies suck milk through

trained taught

vet animal doctor

More books to read

Dog (A Pet's Life), Anita Ganeri (Heinemann Library, 2009)

Dog (Pets in My House), Patricia Whitehouse (Heinemann Library, 2004)

From Puppy to Dog (How Living Things Grow), Anita Ganeri (Heinemann Library, 2006)

Index